This Book Belongs To

....

THE CLASSIC BOOK OF

BEST-LOVED
CHILDREN'S POEMS

THE CLASSIC BOOK OF

BEST-LOVED
CHILDREN'S POEMS

EDITED BY
Virginia Mattingly

WITH ILLUSTRATIONS BY
Nicky Cooney • Robin Lawrie • Graham Percy
Jenny Williams • Rosemary Woods

COURAGE
BOOKS

AN IMPRINT OF RUNNING PRESS
PHILADELPHIA • LONDON

Library of Congress Cataloging-in-Publication Number 96-86290

ISBN 0-7624-0100-1

Cover and interior design by Peter Bennett
Cover illustration by Robin Lawrie
Interior illustrations by Nicky Cooney, Robin Lawrie,
Graham Percy, Jenny Williams, and Rosemary Woods
Edited by Elaine M. Bucher
Set in Caslon

Published by Courage Books, an imprint of
Running Press Book Publishers
125 South Twenty-second Street
Philadelphia, Pennsylvania 19103-4399

FOREWORD

When you look through this book, you shall see
Pages and pages of poetry.
    So find a quiet place,
    And read at your own pace,
As you discover the likes of Blake, Emerson, and Rossetti.

More than forty poems are included in all;
Some pretty big, and some nice and small.
    So whatever your pleasure:
    Little songs or tales of measure,
Here's a perfect collection, spring, winter, summer, or fall.

Pirates, holidays, and animals of all kinds,
Are waiting for you in the nooks of these lines.
    In stories of climbing and adventures of sorts
    You'll visit new places, peoples, and ports.
So travel with us to the magical land of rhyme.

When you're curled in a lap or snuggled in a bed,
Let these poems from all ages dance in your head.
    With Stevenson and Kipling,
    Wordsworth and Browning,
This book will be a favorite each time it is read.

Virginia Mattingly

CONTENTS

CONTENTS

SNAILS AND TAILS

from THE SNAIL

The snail crawls out with his house on his back,
You may know whence he comes by his slimy track.
   Creep, creep, how slowly he goes,
And you'd do the same if you carried your house.

Sabine Baring-Gould

THE SNAIL'S DREAM

A snail, who had a way, it seems,
Of dreaming very curious dreams,
Once dreamed he was—you'll never guess!—
The Lightning Limited Express!

Oliver Herford

THE OWL AND THE PUSSY-CAT

The Owl and the Pussy-Cat went to sea
  In a beautiful pea-green boat;
They took some honey, and plenty of money
  Wrapped up in a five-pound note.
The Owl looked up to the moon above,
  And sang to a small guitar,
"O lovely Pussy! O Pussy, my love!
  What a beautiful Pussy you are,—
    You are,
  What a beautiful Pussy you are!"

Pussy said to the Owl, "You elegant fowl!
  How wonderful sweet you sing!
O let us be married,—too long have we tarried,—
  But what shall we do for a ring?"
They sailed away for a year and a day
  To the land where the Bong-tree grows
And there in a wood, a piggy-wig stood
  With a ring in the end of his nose,—
    His nose,
  With a ring in the end of his nose.

"Dear Pig, are you willing to sell for one shilling
  Your ring?" Said the piggy, "I will."
So they took it away, and were married next day
  By the turkey who lives on the hill.
They dined upon mince and slices of quince,
  Which they ate with a runcible spoon,
And hand in hand on the edge of the sand
  They danced by the light of the moon,—
    The moon,
  They danced by the light of the moon.

Edward Lear

THE FLY-AWAY HORSE

Oh, a wonderful horse is the Fly-Away Horse—
    Perhaps you have seen him before;
    Perhaps, while you slept, his shadow has swept
Through the moonlight that floats on the floor.
For it's only at night, when the stars twinkle bright,
    That the Fly-Away Horse, with a neigh
And a pull at his rein and a toss of his mane,
    Is up on his heels and away!
                    The Moon in the sky,
                    As he gallopeth by,
        Cries: "Oh! what a marvelous sight!"
                    And the Stars in dismay
                    Hide their faces away
        In the lap of old Grandmother Night.

It is yonder, out yonder, the Fly-Away Horse
    Speedeth ever and ever away—
Over meadows and lanes, over mountains and plains,
    Over streamlets that sing at their play;
And over the sea like a ghost sweepeth he,
    While the ships they go sailing below,
And he speedeth so fast that the men at the mast
    Adjudge him some portent of woe.
                    "What ho there!" they cry,
                    As he flourishes by
        With a whisk of his beautiful tail;
                    And the fish in the sea
                    Are as scared as can be,
        From the nautilus up to the whale!

And the Fly-Away Horse seeks those far-away lands
    You little folk dream of at night—
Where candy-trees grow, and honey-brooks flow,
    And corn-fields with popcorn are white;
And the beasts in the wood are ever so good
    To children who visit them there—
What glory astride of a lion to ride,
    Or to wrestle around with a bear!
                The monkeys, they say:
                "Come on, let us play,"
       And they frisk in the cocoanut-trees:
                While the parrots, that cling
                To the peanut-vines, sing
      Or converse with comparative ease!

Off! scamper to bed—you shall ride him to-night!
    For, as soon as you've fallen asleep,
With a jubilant neigh he shall bear you away
    Over forest and hillside and deep!
But tell us, my dear, all you see and you hear
    In those beautiful lands over there,
Where the Fly-Away Horse wings his far-away course
    With the wee one consigned to his care.
                Then grandma will cry
                In amazement: "Oh my!"
       And she'll think it could never be so;
                And only we two
                Shall know it is true—
      You and I, little precious! shall know!

Eugene Field

from THE CAT THAT WALKED BY HIMSELF

Pussy can sit by the fire and sing,
    Pussy can climb a tree,
Or play with a silly old cork and string
    To 'muse herself, not me.
But I like *Binkie* my dog, because
    He knows how to behave;
So, *Binkie's* the same as the First Friend was
    And I am the Man in the Cave. . . .

Pussy will rub my knees with her head.
    Pretending she loves me hard;
But the very minute I go to my bed
    Pussy runs out in the yard,
And there she stays till the morning-light,
    So I know it is only pretend;
But *Binkie*, he snores at my feet all night,
    And he is my Firstest Friend!

Rudyard Kipling

THE CAT OF CATS

I am the cat of cats. I am
  The everlasting cat!
Cunning, and old, and sleek as jam,
  The everlasting cat!
I hunt the vermin in the night—
  The everlasting cat!
For I see best without the light—
  The everlasting cat!

William Brighty Rands

from THE KITTEN AND THE FALLING LEAVES

——But the Kitten, how she starts,
Crouches, stretches, paws, and darts!
First at one, and then its fellow
Just as light and just as yellow;
There are many now—now one—
Now they stop and there are none.
What intenseness of desire
In her upward eye of fire!
With a tiger-leap half-way
Now she meets the coming prey,
Lets it go as fast, and then
Has it in her power again:
Now she works with three or four,
Like an Indian conjurer;
Quick as he in feats of art,
Far beyond in joy of heart.
Were her antics played in the eye
Of a thousand standers-by,
Clapping hands with shout and stare,
What would little Tabby care
For the plaudits of the crowd?
Over happy to be proud,
Over wealthy in the treasure
Of her own exceeding pleasure!

William Wordsworth

MARY'S LAMB

Mary had a little lamb,
    Its fleece was white as snow;
And everywhere that Mary went,
    The lamb was sure to go.

He followed her to school one day,
    Which was against the rule;
It made the children laugh and play
    To see a lamb at school.

And so the teacher turned him out,
    But still he lingered near,
And waited patiently about
    Till Mary did appear.

Then he ran to her, and laid
    His head upon her arm,
As if he said, "I'm not afraid—
    You'll keep me from all harm."

"What makes the lamb love Mary so?"
    The eager children cried.
"Oh, Mary loves the lamb, you know,"
    The teacher quick replied.

And you each gentle animal
    In confidence may bind,
And make them follow at your will,
    If you are only kind.

Sarah Josepha Hale

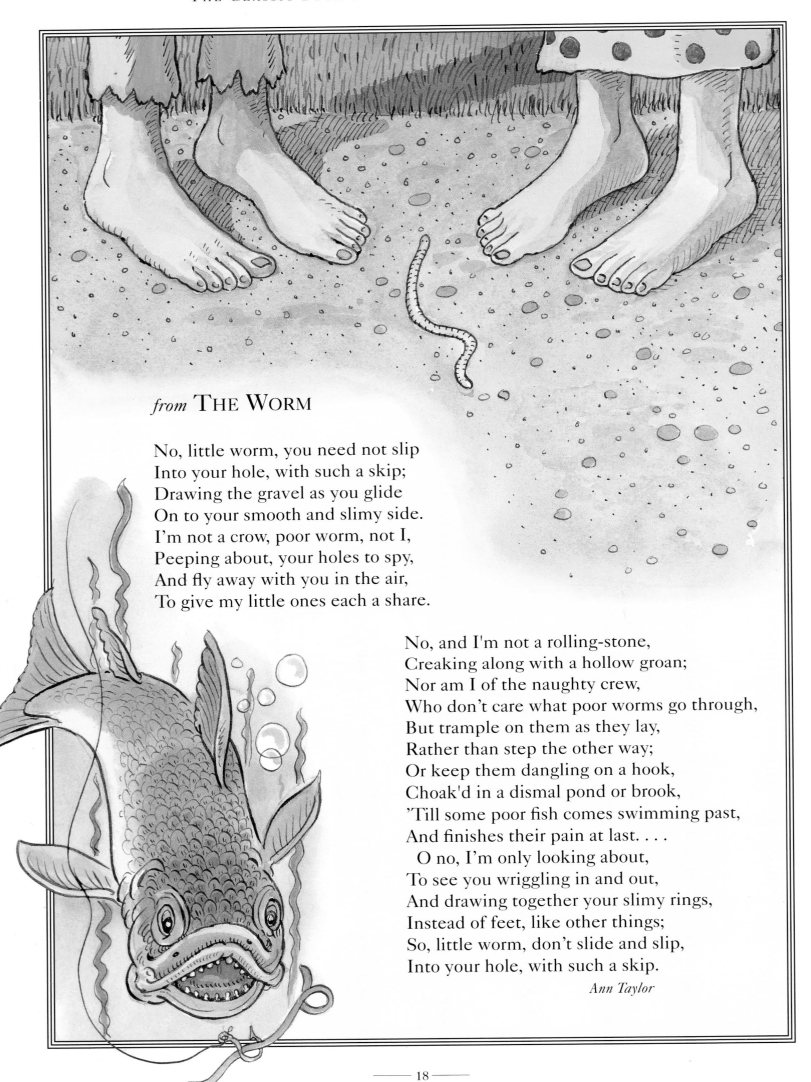

from THE WORM

No, little worm, you need not slip
Into your hole, with such a skip;
Drawing the gravel as you glide
On to your smooth and slimy side.
I'm not a crow, poor worm, not I,
Peeping about, your holes to spy,
And fly away with you in the air,
To give my little ones each a share.

No, and I'm not a rolling-stone,
Creaking along with a hollow groan;
Nor am I of the naughty crew,
Who don't care what poor worms go through,
But trample on them as they lay,
Rather than step the other way;
Or keep them dangling on a hook,
Choak'd in a dismal pond or brook,
'Till some poor fish comes swimming past,
And finishes their pain at last. . . .
  O no, I'm only looking about,
To see you wriggling in and out,
And drawing together your slimy rings,
Instead of feet, like other things;
So, little worm, don't slide and slip,
Into your hole, with such a skip.

Ann Taylor

from THE PELICAN CHORUS

King and Queen of the Pelicans we;
No other Birds so grand we see!
None but we have feet like fins!
With lovely leathery throats and chins!
    Ploffskin, Pluffskin, Pelican jee!
    We think no Birds so happy as we!
    Plumpskin, Ploshkin, Pelican jill!
    We think so then, and we thought so still!

We live on the Nile. The Nile we love.
By night we sleep on the cliffs above;
By day we fish, and at eve we stand
On long bare islands of yellow sand.
And when the sun sinks slowly down
And the great rock walls grow dark and brown,
Where the purple river rolls fast and dim
And the Ivory Ibis starlike skim,
Wing to wing we dance around,—
Stamping our feet with a flumpy sound,—
Opening our mouths as Pelicans ought,
And this is the song we nightly snort;—
    Ploffskin, Pluffskin, Pelican jee,—
    We think no Birds so happy as we!
    Plumpskin, Ploshkin, Pelican jill,—
    We think so then, and we thought so still.

                              Edward Lear

CATERPILLAR

Brown and furry
Caterpillar in a hurry,
Take your walk
To the shady leaf, or stalk,
Or what not,
Which may be the chosen spot.
No toad spy you,
Hovering bird of prey pass by you;
Spin and die,
To live again a butterfly.

Christina Rossetti

from BEASTS, BIRDS, AND FISHES

The Dog will come, when he is call'd,
   The Cat will walk away;
The Monkey's cheek is very bald,
   The Goat is fond of play.
The Parrot is a prate-apace,
   Yet knows not what she says;
The noble Horse will win the race,
   Or draw you in a chaise.

The Pig is not a feeder nice,
   The Squirrel loves a nut;
The Wolf will eat you in a trice,
   The Buzzard's eyes are shut.
The Lark sings high up in the air,
   The Linnet on the tree;
The Swan he has a bosom fair,
   And who so proud as he?

O yes, the Peacock is more proud,
    Because his tail has eyes,
The Lion roars so very loud,
    He fills you with surprise.
The Raven's coat is shining black,
    Or rather raven gray,
The Camel's bunch is on his back,
    The Owl abhors the day.

The Sparrow steals the cherry ripe,
    The Elephant is wise,
The Blackbird charms you with his pipe,
    The false Hyena cries.
The Hen guards well her little chicks,
    The useful Cow is meek,
The Beaver builds with mud and sticks,
    The Lapwing loves to squeak.

The little Wren is very small,
    The Humming Bird is less;
The Lady-bird is least of all,
    And beautiful in dress.
The Pelican she loves her young,
    The Stork his father loves;
The Woodcock's bill is very long,
    And innocent are Doves.

Ann Taylor

LULLABIES

Swing High and Swing Low

Swing high and swing low
While the breezes they blow—
It's off for a sailor thy father would go;
And it's here in the harbor, in sight of the sea,
He hath left his wee babe with my song and with me:
"*Swing high and swing low*
While the breezes they blow!"

Swing high and swing low
While the breezes they blow—
It's oh for the waiting as weary days go!
And it's oh for the heartache that smiteth me when
I sing my song over and over again:
"*Swing high and swing low*
While the breezes they blow!"

"Swing high and swing low"—
The sea singeth so,
And it waileth anon in its ebb and its flow;
And a sleeper sleeps on to that song of the sea
Nor recketh he ever of mine or of me!
"*Swing high and swing low*
While the breezes they blow—
'Twas off for a sailor thy father would go!"

Eugene Field

LULLABY FOR A BABY FAIRY

Night is over; through the clover globes of crystal shine;
Birds are calling; sunlight falling on the wet green vine.
   Little wings must folded lie, little lips be still
   While the sun is in the sky, over Fairy Hill.
      Sleep, sleep, sleep,
         Baby with buttercup hair,
          Golden rays
        Into the violet creep.
    Dream, dream deep;
        Dream of the night-revels fair.
         Daylight stays;
    Sleep, little fairy child, sleep.

Rest in daytime; night is playtime, all good fairies know.
Under sighing grasses lying, off to slumber go.
   Night will come with stars agleam, lilies in her hand,
   Calling you from Hills of Dream back to Fairyland.
      Sleep, sleep, sleep,
         Baby with buttercup hair,
          Golden rays
        Into the violet creep.
    Dream, dream deep;
        Dream of the night-revels fair.
         Daylight stays;
    Sleep, little fairy child, sleep.

Joyce Kilmer

A CRADLE SONG

Golden slumbers kiss your eyes,
Smiles awake you when you rise.
Sleep, pretty wantons, do not cry,
And I will sing a lullaby:
Rock them, rock them, lullaby.

Care is heavy, therefore sleep you;
You are care, and care must keep
    you.
Sleep, pretty wantons, do not cry,
And I will sing a lullaby:
Rock them, rock them, lullaby.

Thomas Dekker

SWEET AND LOW

Sweet and low, sweet and low
    Wind of the western sea,
Low, low, breathe and blow,
    Wind of the western sea!
Over the rolling waters go,
Come from the dying moon, and blow,
    Blow him again to me;
While my little one, while my pretty one, sleeps.

Sleep and rest, sleep and rest,
    Father will come to thee soon;
Rest, rest, on mother's breast,
    Father will come to thee soon;
Father will come to his babe in the nest,
Silver sails all out of the west,
    Under the silver moon;
Sleep, my little one, sleep, my pretty one, sleep.

Alfred, Lord Tennyson

THE WHITE SEAL'S LULLABY

Oh! hush thee, my baby, the night is behind us,
    And black are the waters that sparkled so green.
The moon, o'er the combers, looks downward to find us
    At rest in the hollows that rustle between.

Where billow meets billow, then soft be thy pillow;
    Ah, weary wee flippering, curl at thy ease!
The storm shall not wake thee, nor shark overtake thee,
    Asleep in the arms of the slow-swinging seas.

Rudyard Kipling

from LULLABY, AND GOOD NIGHT

. . . Lullaby, and good night.
You're your mother's delight.
Shining angels beside
My darling abide.
Soft and warm is your bed,
Close your eyes and rest your head.
Soft and warm is your bed,
Close your eyes and rest your head.

Sleepyhead, close your eyes.
Mother's right here beside you.
I'll protect you from harm,
You will wake in my arms.
Guardian angels are near,
So sleep on, with no fear.
Guardian angels are near,
So sleep on, with no fear. . . .

Johannes Brahms

ROCK-A-BYE, BABY

Rock-a-bye, Baby,
In the tree top.
When the wind blows,
The cradle will rock.
When the bough breaks,
The cradle will fall,
And down will come Baby,
Cradle and all.

Baby is drowsing,
Cozy and fair.
Mother sits near,
In her rocking chair.
Forward and back
The cradle she swings,
And though Baby sleeps,
He hears what she sings.

Fom the high rooftops
Down to the sea,
No one's as dear
As baby to me.
Wee little fingers,
Eyes wide and bright—
Now sound asleep
Until morning light.

Traditional lullaby

GOOD NIGHT

Good night! Good night!
Far flies the light;
But still God's love
Shall flame above,
Making all bright.
Good night! Good night!

Victor Hugo

CALL OF THE WILD

TREES

The Oak is called the king of trees,
The Aspen quivers in the breeze,
The Poplar grows up straight and tall,
The Peach tree spreads along the wall,
The Sycamore gives pleasant shade,
The Willow droops in watery glade,
The Fir tree useful timber gives,
The Beech amid the forest lives.

Sara Coleridge

from THE CLOUD

I bring fresh showers for the thirsting flowers,
    From the seas and the streams;
I bear light shade for the leaves when laid
    In their noon-day dreams.
From my wings are shaken the dews that waken
    The sweet buds every one,
When rocked to rest on their mother's breast,
    As she dances about the sun.
I wield the flail of the lashing hail,
    And whiten the green plains under,
And then again I dissolve it in rain,
    And laugh as I pass in thunder.

Percy Bysshe Shelley

from NIGHT

The sun descending in the west,
   The evening star does shine;
The birds are silent in their nest,
   And I must seek for mine.
The moon, like a flower,
In heaven's high bower,
With silent delight
Sits and smiles on the night.

Farewell, green fields and happy groves,
   Where flocks have took delight.
Where lambs have nibbled, silent moves
   The feet of angels bright;
Unseen they pour blessing,
And joy without ceasing,
On each bud and blossom,
And each sleeping bosom.

William Blake

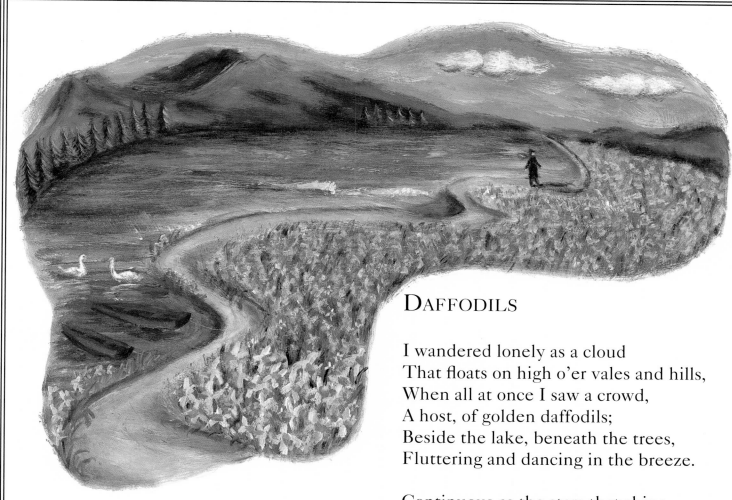

DAFFODILS

I wandered lonely as a cloud
That floats on high o'er vales and hills,
When all at once I saw a crowd,
A host, of golden daffodils;
Beside the lake, beneath the trees,
Fluttering and dancing in the breeze.

Continuous as the stars that shine
And twinkle on the milky way,
They stretched in never-ending line
Along the margin of the bay:
Ten thousand saw I at a glance,
Tossing their heads in sprightly dance.

The waves beside them danced; but they
Out-did the sparkling waves in glee:
A poet could not but be gay,
In such a jocund company:
I gazed—and gazed—but little thought
What wealth the show to me had brought:

For oft, when on my couch I lie
In vacant or in pensive mood,
They flash upon that inward eye
Which is the bliss of solitude;
And then my heart with pleasure fills,
And dances with the daffodils.

William Wordsworth

A CHILL

What can lambkins do
  All the keen night through?
Nestle by their woolly mother,
  The careful ewe.

What can nestlings do
  In the nightly dew?
Sleep beneath their mother's wing
  Till the day breaks anew.

If in field or tree
  There might only be
Such a warm soft sleeping-place
  Found for me!

Christina Rossetti

SEA SHELL

Sea Shell, Sea Shell,
  Sing me a song, O Please!
A song of ships, and sailor men,
  And parrots, and tropical trees,

Of islands lost in the Spanish Main
Which no man ever may find again,
Of fishes and corals under the waves,
And seahorses stabled in great green
  caves.

Sea Shell, Sea Shell,
Sing of the things you know so well.

Amy Lowell

THE CRESCENT MOON

Slipping softly through the sky
　Little horned, happy moon,
Can you hear me up so high?
　Will you come down soon?

On my nursery window-sill
　Will you stay your steady flight?
And then float away with me
　Through the summer night?

Brushing over tops of trees,
　Playing hide and seek with stars,
Peeping up through shiny clouds
　At Jupiter or Mars.

I shall fill my lap with roses
　Gathered in the milky way,
All to carry home to mother.
　Oh! what will she say!

Little rocking, sailing moon,
　Do you hear me shout—Ahoy!
Just a little nearer, moon,
　To please a little boy.

Amy Lowell

TALL TALES & SILLY THINGS

TOPSY-TURVY WORLD

If the butterfly courted the bee,
   And the owl the porcupine;
If churches were built in the sea,
   And three times one were nine;
If the pony rode his master;
   If the buttercups ate the cows;
If the cat had the dire disaster
   To be worried, sir, by the mouse;

If mamma, sir, sold the baby
   To a gipsy for half-a-crown;
If a gentleman, sir, was a lady,—
   The world would be upside-down!
If any or all of these wonders
   Should ever come about,
I should not consider them blunders,
   For I should be inside-out!

William Brighty Rands

I STOOD AGAINST THE WINDOW

I stood against the window
    And looked between the bars,
And there were strings of fairies
    Hanging from the stars;
Everywhere and everywhere
    In shining, swinging chains;
The air was full of shimmering,
    Like sunlight when it rains.

They kept on swinging, swinging,
    They flung themselves so high
They caught upon the pointed moon
    And hung across the sky.
And when I woke next morning,
    There still were crowds and crowds
In beautiful bright bunches
    All sleeping on the clouds.

Rose Fyleman

from THE BEGINNING OF THE ARMADILLOS

. . . I've never seen a Jaguar,
    Nor yet an Armadill—
O dillioing in his armour,
    And I s'pose I never will.

Unless I go to Rio
These wonders to behold—
Roll down—roll down to Rio—
Roll really down to Rio!
Oh, I'd love to roll to Rio
Some day before I'm old!

Rudyard Kipling

WYNKEN, BLYNKEN, AND NOD

Wynken, Blynken, and Nod one night
    Sailed off in a wooden shoe—
Sailed on a river of crystal light,
    Into a sea of dew.
"Where are you going, and what do you wish?"
    The old moon asked the three.
"We have come to fish for the herring fish
    That live in this beautiful sea;
    Nets of silver and gold have we!"
        Said Wynken,
          Blynken,
          And Nod.

The old moon laughed and sang a song,
    As they rocked in the wooden shoe,
And the wind that sped them all night long
    Ruffled the waves of dew.
The little stars were the herring fish
    That lived in that beautiful sea—
"Now cast your nets wherever you wish—
    Never afeard are we";
So cried the stars to the fishermen three:
        Wynken,
        Blynken,
        And Nod.

All night long their nets they threw
    To the stars in the twinkling foam—
Then down from the skies came the wooden shoe,
    Bringing the fishermen home;
'T was all so pretty a sail it seemed
    As if it could not be,
And some folks thought 't was a dream they'd dreamed
    Of sailing that beautiful sea—
    But I shall name you the fishermen three:
                Wynken,
                Blynken,
                And Nod.

Wynken and Blynken are two little eyes,
    And Nod is a little head,
And the wooden shoe that sailed the skies
    Is a wee one's trundle-bed.
So shut your eyes while mother sings
    Of wonderful sights that be,
And you shall see the beautiful things
    As you rock in the misty sea,
    Where the old shoe rocked the fishermen three:
                Wynken,
                Blynken,
                And Nod.

                                Eugene Field

from THE PIED PIPER OF HAMELIN

I

Hamelin Town's in Brunswick,
   By famous Hanover city;
The river Weser, deep and wide,
Washes its walls on the southern side;
A pleasanter spot you never spied;
   But, when begins my ditty,
Almost five hundred years ago,
To see the townsfolk suffer so
   From vermin, was a pity.

II

   Rats!
They fought the dogs and killed the cats
   And bit the babies in the cradles,
And ate the cheeses out of the vats,
And licked the soup from the cooks'
   own ladles,
Split open the kegs of salted sprats,
Made nests inside men's Sunday hats,
And even spoiled the women's chats
   By drowning their speaking
   With shrieking and squeaking
In fifty different sharps and flats.

III

At last the people in a body
 To the Town Hall came flocking:
"'Tis clear," cried they, "our Mayor's a
  noddy;
 And as for our Corporation—shocking
To think we buy gowns lined with ermine
For dolts that can't or won't determine
What's best to rid us of our vermin!
You hope, because you're old and obese,
To find in the furry civic robe ease?
Rouse up, sirs! Give our brains a racking
To find the remedy we're lacking,
Or, sure as fate, we'll send you packing!"
At this the Mayor and Corporation
Quaked with mighty consternation.

IV

An hour they sat in council,
 At length the Mayor broke silence:
"For a guilder I'd my ermine gown sell,
 I wish I were a mile hence!
It's easy to bid one rack one's brain—
I'm sure my poor head aches again,
I've scratched it so, and all in vain.
Oh for a trap, a trap, a trap!"
Just as he said this, what should hap
At the chamber door but a gentle tap?
"Bless us," cried the Mayor, "what's that?"
(With the Corporation as he sat,
Looking little though wondrous fat;
Nor brighter was his eye, nor moister
Than a too-long-opened oyster,
Save when at noon his paunch grew mutinous
For a plate of turtle green and glutinous)
"Only scraping of shoes on the mat?
Anything like the sound of a rat
Makes my heart go pit-a-pat!"

V

"Come in!"—the Mayor cried, looking bigger:
And in did come the strangest figure!
His queer long coat from heel to head
Was half of yellow and half of red,
And he himself was tall and thin,
With sharp blue eyes, each like a pin,
And light loose hair, yet swarthy skin,
No tuft on cheek nor beard on chin,
But lips where smiles went out and in;
There was no guessing his kith and kin:
And nobody could enough admire
The tall man and his quaint attire.
Quoth one: "It's as my great-grandsire,
Starting up at the Trump of Doom's tone,
Had walked this way from his painted tombstone!"

VI

He advanced to the council-table:
And, "Please your honours," said he, "I'm
     able,
By means of a secret charm, to draw
     All creatures living beneath the sun,
     That creep or swim or fly or run,
After me so as you never saw!
And I chiefly use my charm
On creatures that do people harm,
The mole and toad and newt and viper;
And people call me the Pied Piper."
(And here they noticed round his neck

A scarf of red and yellow stripe,
To match with his coat of the self-same cheque;
    And at the scarf's end hung a pipe;
And his fingers, they noticed, were ever straying
As if impatient to be playing
Upon this pipe, as low it dangled
Over his vesture so old-fangled.)
"Yet," said he, "poor piper as I am,
In Tartary I freed the Cham,
    Last June, from his huge swarm of gnats;
I eased in Asia the Nizam
    Of a monstrous brood of vampyre-bats:
And as for what your brain bewilders,
    If I can rid your town of rats
Will you give me a thousand guilders?"
"One? fifty thousand!"—was the exclamation
Of the astonished Mayor and Corporation.

VII

Into the street the Piper stept,
    Smiling first a little smile,
As if he knew what magic slept
    In his quiet pipe the while;
Then, like a musical adept,
To blow the pipe his lips he wrinkled,
And green and blue his sharp eyes twinkled,
Like a candle flame where salt is sprinkled;
And ere three shrill notes the pipe uttered,
You heard as if an army muttered;
And the muttering grew to a grumbling;
And the grumbling grew to a mighty rumbling;
And out of the houses the rats came tumbling.
Great rats, small rats, lean rats, brawny rats,
Brown rats, black rats, gray rats, tawny rats,
Grave old plodders, gay young friskers,
    Fathers, mothers, uncles, cousins,
Cocking tails and pricking whiskers,
    Families by tens and dozens,
Brothers, sisters, husbands, wives—
Followed the Piper for their lives.

Robert Browning

PIRATE STORY

Three of us afloat in the meadow by the swing,
   Three of us aboard in the basket on the lea.
Winds are in the air, they are blowing in the spring,
   And waves are on the meadow like the waves there are at sea.

Where shall we adventure, to-day that we're afloat,
   Wary of the weather and steering by a star?
Shall it be to Africa, a-steering of the boat,
   To Providence, or Babylon, or off to Malabar?

Hi! but here's a squadron a-rowing on the sea—
   Cattle on the meadow a-charging with a roar!
Quick, and we'll escape them, they're as mad as they can be,
   The wicket is the harbor and the garden is the shore.

Robert Louis Stevenson

THE LAND OF STORY-BOOKS

At evening when the lamp is lit,
Around the fire my parents sit;
They sit at home and talk and sing,
And do not play at anything.

Now, with my little gun, I crawl
All in the dark along the wall,
And follow round the forest track
Away behind the sofa back.

There, in the night, where none can spy,
All in my hunter's camp I lie,
  And play at books that I have read
  Till it is time to go to bed.

These are the hills, these are the woods,
These are my starry solitudes;
And there the river by whose brink
The roaring lions come to drink.

I see the others far away
As if in firelit camp they lay,
And I, like to an Indian scout,
Around their party prowled about.

So, when my nurse comes in for me,
Home I return across the sea,
And go to bed with backward looks
At my dear Land of Story-books.

Robert Louis Stevenson

A Nonsense Rhyme

Ringlety-jing!
And what will we sing?
Some little crinkety-crankety thing
That rhymes and chimes,
And skips, sometimes,
As though wound up with a kink in the spring.

Grunkety-krung!
And chunkety-plung!
Sing the song that the bullfrog sung,—
A song of the soul
Of a mad tadpole
That met his fate in a leaky bowl:
And it's O for the first false wiggle he made
In a sea of pale pink lemonade!
And it's O for the thirst
Within him pent,
And the hopes that burst
As his reason went—
When his strong arm failed and his strength was spent!

Sing, O sing
Of the things that cling,
And the claws that clutch and the fangs that sting—
Till the tadpole's tongue
And his tail upflung
Quavered and failed with a song unsung!
O the dank despair in the rank morass,
Where the crawfish crouch in the cringing grass,
And the long limp rune of the loon wails on
For the mad, sad soul
Of a bad tadpole
Forever lost and gone!

Jinglety-jee!
And now we'll see
What the last of the lay shall be,
As the dismal tip of the tune, O friends,
Swoons away and the long tale ends.
And it's O and alack!
For the tangled legs
And the spangled back
Of the green grig's eggs,
And the unstrung strain
Of the strange refrain
That the winds wind up like a strand of rain!

And it's O
Also
For the ears wreathed low,
Like a laurel-wreath on the lifted brow
Of the frog that cants of the why and how
And the wherefore too, and the thus and so
Of the wail he weaves in a woof of woe!
Twangle, then, with your wrangling strings,
The tinkling links of a thousand things!
And clang the pang of a maddening moan
Till the Echo, hid in a land unknown,
Shall leap as he hears, and hoot and hoo
Like the wretched wraith of a Whoopty-Doo!

James Whitcomb Riley

MINNIE AND WINNIE

Minnie and Winnie
Slept in a shell.
Sleep, little ladies!
And they slept well.

Pink was the shell within,
Silver without;
Sounds of the great sea
Wandered about.

Sleep, little ladies!
Wake not soon!
Echo on echo
Dies to the moon.

Two bright stars
Peeped into the shell.
"What are they dreaming of?
Who can tell?"

Startled a green linnet
Out of the croft;
Wake, little ladies!
The sun is aloft.

Alfred, Lord Tennyson

MERRY MELODIES

THE BLUEBIRD

I know the song that the bluebird is singing,
Out in the apple-tree where he is swinging.
Brave little fellow! the skies may be dreary,—
Nothing cares he while his heart is so cheery.

Hark! how the music leaps out from his throat!
Hark! was there ever so merry a note?
Listen a while, and you'll hear what he's saying,
Up in the apple-tree swinging and swaying.

"Dear little blossoms down under the snow,
You must be weary of winter, I know;
Hark while I sing you a message of cheer!
Summer is coming, and spring-time is here!

"Little white snow-drop! I pray you arise;
Bright yellow crocus! come open your eyes;
Sweet little violets, hid from the cold,
Put on your mantles of purple and gold;
Daffodils! daffodils! say, do you hear?—
Summer is coming! and spring-time is here!"

Emily Huntington Miller

TWINKLE, TWINKLE, LITTLE STAR

Twinkle, twinkle, little star,
How I wonder what you are!
Up above the world so high,
Like a diamond in the sky.

 Twinkle, twinkle, little star,
 How I wonder what you are!

When the blazing sun goes down,
Darkness falls all over town.
Then you show your tiny light,
Twinkling, twinkling through the night.

 Twinkle, twinkle, little star,
 How I wonder what you are!

Weary travelers in the dark
Thank you for your little spark.
Who could see which path to go,
If you did not twinkle so?

 Twinkle, twinkle, little star,
 How I wonder what you are!

In the dark sky you remain,
Peeking through the windowpane,
And you never shut your eye
'Til the sun is in the sky.

 Twinkle, twinkle, little star,
 How I wonder what you are!

As your bright and tiny spark
Lights the traveler in the dark,
Though I know not what you are,
Twinkle, twinkle, little star!

 Twinkle, twinkle, little star,
 How I wonder what you are!

Jane Taylor

THE PIPER

Piping down the valleys wild,
  Piping songs of pleasant glee,
On a cloud I saw a child;
  And he, laughing, said to me,

"Pipe a song about a lamb!"
  So I piped with merry cheer.
"Piper, pipe that song again!"
  So I piped; he wept to hear.

"Drop thy pipe, thy happy pipe;
  Sing thy songs of happy cheer!"
So I sang the same again,
  While he wept with joy to hear.

"Piper, sit thou down, and write
  In a book, that all may read!"
So he vanished from my sight,
  And I plucked a hollow reed,

And I made a rural pen,
  And I stained the water clear;
And I wrote my happy songs
  Every child may joy to hear.

William Blake

from THE NEW-ENGLAND BOY'S SONG
ABOUT THANKSGIVING DAY

Over the river, and through the wood,
　　To grandfather's house we go;
　　　　The horse knows the way,
　　　　To carry the sleigh,
　　Through the white and drifted snow.

Over the river, and through the wood,
　　To grandfather's house away!
　　　　We would not stop
　　　　For doll or top,
　　For 't is Thanksgiving day.

Over the river, and through the wood,
　　Oh, how the wind does blow!
　　　　It stings the toes,
　　　　And bites the nose,
　　As over the ground we go.

Over the river, and through the wood,
　　With a clear blue winter sky,
　　　　The dogs do bark,
　　　　And children hark,
　　As we go jingling by.

Over the river, and through the wood,
To have a first-rate play—
Hear the bells ring
Ting a ling ding,
Hurra for Thanksgiving day!

Over the river, and through the wood—
No matter for winds that blow;
Or if we get
The sleigh upset,
Into a bank of snow. . . .

Over the river, and through the wood,
Trot fast, my dapple grey!
Spring over the ground,
Like a hunting hound,
For 't is Thanksgiving day!

Over the river, and through the wood,
And straight through the barn-yard gate;
We seem to go
Extremely slow,
It is so hard to wait.

Over the river, and through the wood—
Old Jowler hears our bells;
He shakes his pow,
With a loud bow wow,
And thus the news he tells.

Over the river, and through the wood—
When grandmother sees us come,
She will say, Oh dear,
The children are here,
Bring a pie for every one.

Over the river, and through the wood—
Now grandmother's cap I spy!
Hurra for the fun!
Is the pudding done?
Hurra for the pumpkin pie!

L. Maria Child

MARCHING SONG

Bring the comb and play upon it!
   Marching, here we come!
Willie cocks his highland bonnet,
   Johnnie beats the drum.

Mary Jane commands the party,
   Peter leads the rear;
Feet in time, alert and hearty,
   Each a Grenadier!

All in the most martial manner
   Marching double-quick;
While the napkin like a banner
   Waves upon the stick!

Here's enough of fame and pillage,
   Great commander Jane!
Now that we've been round the village,
   Let's go home again.
            Robert Louis Stevenson

PLAYFUL RHYMES

CLIMBING

High up in the apple tree climbing I go,
With the sky above me, the earth below.
Each branch is the step of a wonderful stair
Which leads to the town I see shining up there.

Climbing, climbing, higher and higher,
The branches blow and I see a spire,
The gleam of a turret, the glint of a dome,
All sparkling and bright, like white sea foam.

On and on, from bough to bough,
The leaves are thick, but I push my way through;
Before, I have always had to stop,
But to-day I am sure I shall reach the top.

Today to the end of the marvelous stair,
Where those glittering pinacles flash in the air!
Climbing, climbing, higher I go,
With the sky close above me, the earth far below.

Amy Lowell

THE CHILDREN'S HOUR

Between the dark and the daylight,
    When the night is beginning to lower,
Comes a pause in the day's occupations,
    That is known as the Children's Hour.

I hear in the chamber above me
    The patter of little feet,
The sound of a door that is opened,
    And voices soft and sweet.

From my study I see in the lamplight,
    Descending the broad hall stair,
Grave Alice, and laughing Allegra,
    And Edith with golden hair.

A whisper, and then a silence:
    Yet I know by their merry eyes
They are plotting and planning together
    To take me by surprise.

A sudden rush from the stairway,
    A sudden raid from the hall!
By three doors left unguarded
    They enter my castle wall!

They climb up into my turret
    O'er the arms and back of my chair;
If I try to escape, they surround me;
    They seem to be everywhere.

They almost devour me with kisses,
    Their arms about me entwine,
Till I think of the Bishop of Bingen
    In his Mouse-Tower on the Rhine!

Do you think, O blue-eyed banditti,
    Because you have scaled the wall,
Such an old mustache as I am
    Is not a match for you all!

I have you fast in my fortress,
  And will not let you depart,
But put you down into the dungeon
  In the round-tower of my heart.

And there I will keep you forever,
  Yes, forever and a day,
Till the walls shall crumble to ruin,
  And moulder in dust away!

Henry Wadsworth Longfellow

CHILD'S TALK IN APRIL

I wish you were a pleasant wren,
  And I your small accepted mate;
How we'd look down on toilsome men!
  We'd rise and go to bed at eight
  Or it may be not quite so late.

Then you should see the nest I'd build,
  The wondrous nest for you and me;
The outside rough, perhaps, but filled
  With wool and down: ah, you should see
  The cosey nest that it would be.

We'd have our change of hope and fear,
  Small quarters, reconcilements sweet:
I'd perch by you to chirp and cheer,
  Or hop about on active feet
  And fetch you dainty bits to eat.

We'd be so happy by the day,
  So safe and happy through the night,
We both should feel, and I should say,
  It's all one season of delight,
And we'll make merry whilst we may.

Christina Rossetti

from BY THE WATER

There are rivers lapsing down
    Lily-laden to the sea:
Every lily is a boat
    For bees, one, two, or three:
I wish there were a fairy boat
    For you, my friend, and me.

Christina Rossetti

MY LITTLE DOLL

I once had a sweet little doll, dears,
    The prettiest doll in the world;
Her cheeks were so red and so white, dears,
    And her hair was so charmingly curled.
But I lost my poor little doll, dears,
    As I played in the heath one day;
And I cried for more than a week, dears,
    But I never could find where she lay.

I found my poor little doll, dears,
    As I played in the heath one day;
Folks say she is terribly changed, dears,
    For her paint is all washed away,
And her arms trodden off by the cows, dears,
    And her hair not the least bit curled:
Yet for old sakes' sake she is still, dears,
    The prettiest doll in the world.

Charles Kingsley

CHUSING A NAME

I have got a new-born sister;
I was nigh the first that kiss'd
  her.
When the nursing woman brought
  her
To Papa, his infant daughter,
How Papa's dear eyes did glisten!—
She will shortly be to christen:
And Papa has made the offer,

I shall have the naming of her.
Now I wonder what would please
    her,
Charlotte, Julia, or Louisa.
Ann and Mary, they're too common;
Joan's too formal for a woman. . . .
They would say, if 'twas Rebecca,
That she was a little Quaker.
Edith's pretty, but that looks
Better in old English books;
Ellen's left off long ago;
Blanche is out of fashion now.
None that I have nam'd as yet
Are so good as Margaret.
Emily is neat and fine.
What do you think of Caroline?
How I'm puzzled and perplext
What to chuse or think of next!
I am in a little fever.
Lest the name that I shall give her
Should disgrace her or defame her
I will leave Papa to name her.

Charles Lamb

The Circus-Day Parade

Oh! the Circus-Day Parade! How the
bugles played and played!
And how the glossy horses tossed their
flossy manes and neighed,
As the rattle and the rhyme of the
tenor-drummer's time
Filled all the hungry hearts of us with
melody sublime!

How the grand band-wagon shone with a splendor all its own,
And glittered with a glory that our dreams had never known!
And how the boys behind, high and low of every kind,
Marched in unconscious capture, with a rapture undefined!

How the horsemen, two and two, with their plumes of white and blue,
And crimson, gold and purple, nodding by at me and you,
Waved the banners that they bore, as the knights in days of yore,
Till our glad eyes gleamed and glistened like the spangles that they wore!

How the graceless-graceful stride of the elephant was eyed,
And the capers of the little horse that cantered at his side!
How the shambling camels, tame to the plaudits of their fame,
With listless eyes came silent, masticating as they came.

How the cages jolted past, with each wagon battened fast,
And the mystery within it only hinted of at last
From the little grated square in the rear, and nosing there
The snout of some strange animal that sniffed the outer air!

And, last of all, The Clown, making mirth for all the town,
With his lips curved ever upward and his eyebrows ever down,
And his chief attention paid to the little mule that played
A tattoo on the dash-board with his heels, in the Parade.

Oh! the Circus-Day Parade! How the bugles played and played!
And how the glossy horses tossed their flossy manes and neighed,
As the rattle and the rhyme of the tenor-drummer's time
Filled all the hungry hearts of us with melody sublime!

James Whitcomb Riley